C000181792

PAUL HARTLEY

The Marvellous

MINIATURE

MARMITE

COOKBOOK

A.

First published in Great Britain in 2012 by
Absolute Press, an imprint of Bloomsbury Publishing Plc
Scarborough House, 29 James Street West
Bath BA1 2BT, England
Phone +44 (0)1225 316013 **Fax** +44 (0)1225 445836
E-mail info@absolutepress.co.uk **Web** www.absolutepress.co.uk

Publisher Jon Croft **Commissionig Editor** Meg Avent
Art Direction Matt Inwood **Design** Matt Inwood and Claire Siggery

A catalogue record of this book is available from the British Library
ISBN 13: 9781906650544

Printed in China by C&C Offset Printing Co. Ltd

Bloomsbury Publishing Plc
50 Bedford Square, London WC1B 3DP I www.bloomsbury.com

Contents

An Introduction

Nine
PURÉE
Ten
WRAP
Eleven
PIZZA
Twelve
JACKETS
Thirteen
NOODLES
Fourteen
RUB
Fifteen
VEGETABLES
Sixteen
CHEESECAKE

Seventeen
RISOTTO
Eighteen
LOAF SANDWICH
Nineteen
ROASTIES
Twenty
CANAPÉS
Twenty-one
PÂTÉ
Twenty-two
BEANS
Twenty-three
ONIONS
Twenty-four
VINAIGRETTE

Twenty-five
POPCORN

Twenty-six
PITTA

Twenty-seven
PANCAKES

Twenty-eight
BURGERS

Twenty-nine
FRENCH TOAST

Thirty
RAREBIT

Thirty-one
PASTA

Thirty-two
TOFU

Thirty-three
SOUP

Thirty-four
MUSHROOMS

Thirty-five
YORKIES

Thirty-six
CROUTONS

Thirty-seven
BANG BANG

Thirty-eight
SALSA

Thirty-nine
BAGELS

Forty
CRISPS

An introduction

A note on oven temperatures
The recipes in this book have been created using a fan-assisted oven.
If you're using a conventional oven, be prepared to add about 10 degrees to
the temperatures given and allow up to a few extra minutes of cooking time
to achieve the desired result.

Many people take Marmite from their cupboards once every day, first thing in the morning. They nestle it in the middle of the breakfast table, along with jams and butter and cereal and milk. Some will reach for Marmite and only Marmite. Satéd with a wonderful savoury slice of toast or a gloriously enhanced half of muffin, that beautiful little pot then gets returned to the cupboard ready to come out again 24 hours later.

IT NEED NOT BE THIS WAY...

It's the aim of this miniature but ambitious book to persuade you of the merits of bringing Marmite out of the cupboard more than just that once. It enriches so much beyond the breaded products of breakfast. It enhances soups, gravies, meats, sauces and pasta, to name but a few. It is a little pot that deserves more than just ten short minutes of daylight. It should be on round-the-clock release, for it is nothing short of indispensable.

IT REALLY IS QUITE MARVELLOUS.

Now, go forth and experiment...

One

SCRAMBLE

★

Gives eggs a beating they won't forget.

A perfect, quick and healthy breakfast for people in a hurry. Pour a glass of orange juice to go with it and you have a vitamin-packed breakfast to give you fuel for the day.

FOR BREAKFAST FOR 2, WHISK UP 4 LARGE FREE-RANGE EGGS AND SEASON WITH A LITTLE PEPPER. TOAST AND BUTTER 2 SLICES OF BREAD AND SPREAD WITH YOUR DESIRED AMOUNT OF **MARMITE**. ADD A KNOB OF BUTTER TO A NON-STICK PAN AND SCRAMBLE THE EGGS UNTIL SOFT AND CREAMY. POUR OVER THE MARMITE TOAST AND START YOUR DAY **THE MARMITE WAY**.

Two

{ SAUCE }

★

Making sauce just that little bit saucier.

Cheesy sauces are great to perk up vegetables, pour over pasta and cheer up chicken or liven up leftovers. This is a quick and easy supper to feed the family on weekday nights.

MELT 25G OF UNSALTED BUTTER IN A SAUCEPAN, ADD 30G OF PLAIN FLOUR AND COOK TO A PASTE, STIRRING FOR 2 MINUTES. ADD 450ML OF WARM MILK, 60G GRATED CHEESE AND A TEASPOON OF **MARMITE**. STIR UNTIL A THICK SAUCE. COOK 300G OF MACARONI AS PACKET INSTRUCTIONS, DRAIN AND POUR INTO AN OVEN DISH. CHOP UP YOUR LEFTOVER CHICKEN, SCATTER OVER THE PASTA AND POUR THE CHEESY SAUCE OVER IT ALL. POP UNDER A HOT GRILL FOR 4–5 MINUTES AND THE JOB'S A GOOD'N.

Three

DIP

★

Chop. Dip. Munch.

Dips make great party food or easy starters and are a great way to get the kids to eat some of their 5-a-day if you give them raw vegetables to munch with their favourite dip.

FOR 4 PEOPLE, MIX TOGETHER A 250G TUB OF MASCARPONE CHEESE, A TEASPOON OF **MARMITE**, A TABLESPOON OF CHOPPED FRESH CHIVES AND A GRIND OF BLACK PEPPER. TAKE 1 LARGE CARROT, 2 STICKS OF CELERY, 1 DESEEDED SWEET RED PEPPER AND SOME FLORETS OF CAULIFLOWER AND CUT, RAW, INTO FINGER-SIZED PIECES. ARRANGE ON A PLATE AROUND A BOWL OF THE DIP AND GET THE FAMILY DIPPING AND MUNCHING.

Four

STUFFING

★

It's well worth getting your hands dirty.

Stuffing balls are not just for roast dinners.
Serve them with chicken, pork chops, steaks
– anything you fancy. This easy recipe will feed a
large family or you can freeze some for next time.

FINELY CHOP 1 MEDIUM ONION AND FRY
IN 40G OF BUTTER UNTIL SOFT. ADD IN A
HANDFUL OF FINELY CHOPPED DRIED
APRICOTS, BLACK PEPPER AND A GOOD
PINCH OF DRIED HERBS. STIR IN A
TEASPOON OF **MARMITE**, BLEND WELL
AND ADD IN 200G OF FRESH WHITE
BREADCRUMBS, STIR AND REMOVE FROM
THE HEAT. HANDS ONLY –
MAKE MINI OR MAXI BALLS.
BAKE AT 180C/GAS 4 FOR 15 MINUTES.

Five

GRAVY

★

Meat and two veg demand it.

For the next Sunday roast give the family a real treat with this gorgeous gravy, flavoured with their favourite yeast extract. Simple to do but makes a real difference.

WHEN YOU HAVE ROASTED YOUR SUNDAY JOINT, REMOVE IT FROM THE PAN TO REST. DRAIN OFF EXCESS FAT FROM THE PAN, LEAVING BEHIND ALL THE JUICES AND CRISPY BITS. TIP IN A SMALL GLASS OF RED WINE, THEN ADD A TABLESPOON OF FLOUR AND A GOOD TEASPOON OF **MARMITE** AND STIR RAPIDLY. HEAT ON THE HOB, STILL STIRRING, BRING IT TO THE BOIL AND REDUCE JUST A LITTLE TO BURN OFF THE ALCOHOL. *ET VOILÀ*: GORGEOUS GRAVY IN A MATTER OF MOMENTS.

Six

MUFFINS

★

Very respectably English.

English muffins make a great breakfast or brunch and you can pile all sorts of things on top to vary the menu. Check out this veggie option (although it's far too good for vegetarians to keep this to themselves).

FOR 2 PEOPLE WILT 150G OF FRESH WASHED BABY LEAF SPINACH BY POURING A KETTLE OF BOILING WATER OVER IT. DRAIN, STIR IN 2 TEASPOONS OF **MARMITE** AND KEEP WARM. SPLIT, TOAST AND BUTTER 2 MUFFINS AND SOFT-POACH 4 EGGS. PILE THE SPINACH ON EACH MUFFIN HALF AND TOP WITH THE POACHED EGGS. PERFECT.

Seven

ROSTI

★

They taste grate.

Rösti are surprisingly easy to make and incredibly versatile. You can use regular potatoes or sweet potatoes. Try piling leftover strips of rare beef on top, adding a handful of dressed leaves and a dip of horseradish mayonnaise.

PEEL AND GRATE 2 LARGE POTATOES AND 1 MEDIUM ONION INTO A BOWL. ADD HALF A TEASPOON OF PAPRIKA, 1 TABLESPOON OF CHOPPED PARSLEY, 2 EGGS AND A GOOD GRIND OF BLACK PEPPER PLUS 2 TEASPOONS OF **MARMITE**. NOW GET MESSY AND MIX TOGETHER BY HAND AND FORM 2 EVEN PATTIES. BRING 25G OF BUTTER AND A TABLESPOON OF OIL TO A SIZZLE IN A FRYING PAN AND SLIDE IN THE ROSTI. FRY UNTIL GOLDEN. THEN POP INTO THE OVEN FOR 10 MINUTES AT 180C/GAS 4 WHILE YOU PREPARE THE TOPPING.

Eight

GLAZE

★

Go on, finish it off the Marmite way.

Next time you boil a gammon joint, try finishing it off in the oven with a luscious glaze and then serve the ham warm or cold. You'll never cook it any other way again!

FOR A 1.5KG GAMMON JOINT, BOIL THEN SIMMER FOR 1 HOUR IN WATER WITH A TABLESPOON OF BROWN SUGAR AND A FEW PEPPERCORNS. REMOVE AND PLACE IN A BAKING TIN LINED WITH FOIL. WARM 2 LARGE TABLESPOONS OF MARMALADE IN A SAUCEPAN AND STIR IN A TEASPOON OF **MARMITE**. REMOVE FROM THE HEAT AND COOL A LITTLE. NOW PASTE IT ALL OVER THE COOKED HAM AND COOK IN A HOT OVEN FOR 15–20 MINUTES UNTIL GOLDEN.

Nine

PURÉE

★

A silky carroty wonder of a thing.

Chopped into dice or batons, steamed, boiled or roasted: for a change how about some delicious creamy purée – made extra-special with **Marmite**.

FOR 2–3 GOOD-SIZED PORTIONS, PEEL 3 LARGE CARROTS AND DICE INTO SMALL CUBES. PUT INTO A PAN OF BOILING WATER WITH A LEVEL TABLESPOON OF DEMERARA SUGAR AND BOIL FOR 15 MINUTES UNTIL VERY SOFT. DRAIN AND PUT IN A BLENDER WITH 2 TEASPOONS OF **MARMITE**, 2 TABLESPOONS OF DOUBLE CREAM, A PINCH OF GROUND NUTMEG AND A GRIND OF BLACK PEPPER. BLITZ UNTIL YOU HAVE A SMOOTH, CREAMY PURÉE.

Ten

WRAP

★

A hand-held boot for the taste buds.

Wraps are wonderful vehicles for whatever takes your fancy; perfect for a packed lunch or an instant meal. Soft flour tortillas can be stored in the freezer and just brought out and warmed as you need them.

FOR EACH PERSON, TAKE 1 TORTILLA AND SPREAD IT WITH YOUR DESIRED AMOUNT OF **MARMITE** THEN LAY ON SOME SLICED COOKED CHICKEN AND HALF AN AVOCADO (PEELED, STONED AND SLICED), A HANDFUL OF ROCKET AND A DOLLOP OF MAYONNAISE. THEN WRAP IT UP AND DEVOUR !

Eleven

PIZZA

★

Mamma mia, Marmite.

You can always create a great pizza with odds and ends left over in the fridge so keep some bases in the freezer for when you need a quick and easy supper. Otherwise, a quick trip to the deli will get you just what you want for this one.

TO MAKE 1 PIZZA. SPREAD THE BASE WITH **MARMITE** AND THEN ADD DOLLOPS OF TOMATO PURÉE OVER IT. ARRANGE SOME THINLY SLICED CHORIZO, SOME SLICED TOMATO, A FEW SLICED MUSHROOMS, A SCATTERING OF CHOPPED OLIVES AND A FEW TORN BASIL LEAVES OVER THE PIZZA. FINISH WITH SOME SLICED OR GRATED MOZZARELLA AND A DRIZZLE OF OLIVE OIL. POP INTO A HOT OVEN FOR 10 MINUTES AND YOU'RE READY FOR A TASTE OF THE MEDITERRANEAN.

Twelve

JACKETS

★

Potatoes with pow!

Jacket potatoes are a real family favourite and
a good winter warmer.

TO FEED 4 HUNGRY PEOPLE TAKE 4
BAKING POTATOES, RUB ALL OVER WITH
OLIVE OIL AND SPRINKLE WITH SEA SALT.
BAKE IN THE OVEN FOR 45MINS- 1 HOUR
AT 180C/GAS 4 UNTIL CRISPY OUTSIDE
AND YIELDING TO A SQUEEZE. CUT A
CROSS IN THE TOP OF EACH AND SQUEEZE
TO OPEN THEM UP. ADD A PROPER KNOB
OF BUTTER TO EACH AND AS IT MELTS
SPREAD IN THE **MARMITE**. SPOON OVER
SOME WARM BAKED BEANS AND ADD A
HANDFUL OF GRATED CHEESE. POP THEM
BACK IN THE OVEN TO MELT THE CHEESE,
REMOVE, SERVE, AND DIG IN.

Thirteen

NOODLES

★

Chop chop.

Everybody loves a stir fry and **Marmite** adds
a real depth of flavour to your favourite combination
of meat and vegetables.

FOR 2 PEOPLE. HEAT YOUR WOK OR
FRYING PAN AND ADD A GOOD SPLOSH
OF SESAME OIL. HEAT THE PAN TO 'JUST-
SMOKING' AND ADD A HANDFUL EACH OF
ANY OF THE FOLLOWING, EITHER DICED
OR CHOPPED: SPRING ONIONS, SWEET
PEPPER, MUSHROOMS, BABY CORN,
MANGE TOUT, BROCCOLI, CABBAGE,
BEANSPROUTS, BEEF, CHICKEN, PORK!
STIR IN A TEASPOON OF **MARMITE** AND A
GOOD DOLLOP OF SWEET CHILLI SAUCE.
STIR-FRY QUICKLY, KEEPING A CRUNCH
TO THE VEGETABLES AND TOSS IN SOME
FRESH NOODLES. TURN THEM OVER A FEW
TIMES UNTIL HOT AND SERVE.

Fourteen

❧ RUB ❧

★

Rub-a-dub-dub.

Giving the skin of the meat a flavour rub, especially chicken, adds taste and crispness to the finished roast. This recipe is packed with big flavours.

FOR 1 MEDIUM ROAST CHICKEN, GENTLY WARM 1 TABLESPOON OF **MARMITE** IN A MICROWAVE OR SAUCEPAN TO MAKE IT 'PAINTABLE'. ZEST 1 LEMON AND PICK THE LEAVES OFF A GOOD SPRIG OF FRESH THYME, THEN MIX THE TWO TOGETHER. PAINT THE BIRD ALL OVER WITH MARMITE. NOW FOR THE MESSY BIT: USE BOTH HANDS TO RUB THE LEMON-THYME MIXTURE INTO THE MARMITE-COATED SKIN. ROAST AS NORMAL, COVERED WITH FOIL UNTIL THE LAST 15 MINUTES. CRISPY SKIN, SOFT MOIST CHICKEN – DIVINE.

Fifteen

VEGETABLES

★

Rootin'-tootin', finger-lickin' good.

Root vegetables can be a little bland to some palates but roasting with a little **Marmite** brings them to life as an easy side dish, perfect with roasts and casseroles.

FOR 4 PEOPLE, PEEL AND CHUNK 2 MEDIUM PARSNIPS, 2 LARGE CARROTS, 2 MEDIUM POTATOES, ALONG WITH A DOZEN SMALL WHOLE SHALLOTS. PUT 2 TABLESPOONS OF VEGETABLE OIL INTO A ROASTING PAN AND HEAT IN THE OVEN AT 180C/GAS 4 FOR 5 MINUTES. REMOVE, CAREFULLY STIR IN A TABLESPOON OF **MARMITE** THEN ADD ALL THE VEGETABLES. TURN THEM IN THE OIL TO COAT AND RETURN THE PAN TO THE OVEN FOR 45 MINUTES. JUST BEFORE SERVING, ADD A GOOD GRIND OF BLACK PEPPER.

Sixteen

CHEESECAKE

★

Marmite cheesecake? Is nothing sacred?

We don't always think of cheesecake as a savoury dish but it does lend itself to all sorts of savoury fillings, especially **Marmite**.

TO SERVE 4, LINE A DEEP 20CM FLAN TIN WITH SHORTCRUST PASTRY AND CHILL. IN A BOWL, BEAT TOGETHER 125G OF CREAM CHEESE, 125G OF FROMAGE FRAIS, 3 EGGS AND 1 TABLESPOON OF **MARMITE**. DICE 2 RASHERS OF BACON AND SLICE 1 MEDIUM RED ONION AND SAUTÉ FOR A FEW MINUTES. LIFT OUT WITH A SLOTTED SPOON AND ADD TO THE CHEESE MIXTURE. TIP INTO THE PASTRY CASE AND BAKE FOR 90 MINUTES AT 160C/GAS 3 UNTIL SET AND JUST GOLDEN. LEAVE TO COOL A LITTLE AND SERVE WITH A CRISPY GREEN SALAD.

Seventeen

RISOTTO

Storecupboard heaven.

Don't be put off by thinking risotto is tricky because it's not. It just needs a little patience and attention – it's actually even therapeutic after a busy day.

DISSOLVE 3 TABLESPOONS OF **MARMITE** IN 1 PINT OF BOILING WATER. FINELY DICE 2 LARGE SHALLOTS AND 1 CLOVE OF GARLIC AND PREPARE 1 TEASPOON OF FRESH THYME LEAVES AND THE ZEST OF 1 LEMON. MELT 25G OF BUTTER IN A HEAVY-BASED PAN, SAUTÉ THE SHALLOTS AND GARLIC UNTIL SOFT THEN ADD THE THYME AND ZEST. OVER A LOW-MEDIUM HEAT, ADD RISOTTO RICE SUCH AS ARBORIO AND SAUTÉ UNTIL TRANSPARENT, THEN GRADUALLY ADD THE MARMITE STOCK, EACH TIME WAITING FOR THE RICE TO ABSORB IT BEFORE ADDING MORE AND STIRRING ALL THE TIME. YOU MAY NOT NEED ALL THE STOCK – JUST STOP WHEN *AL DENTE*. FINISH WITH A SPLASH OF CREAM, A FEW SLICED SAUTÉED MUSHROOMS, SEASON AND SERVE.

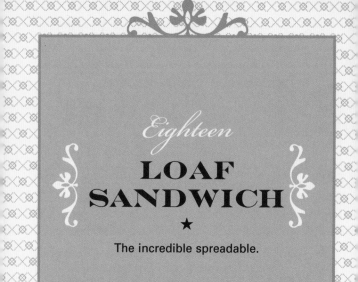

Eighteen

LOAF SANDWICH

★

The incredible spreadable.

This is a great way to make sandwiches with a difference to feed 4 people. The filling can be any combination of your choice but **Marmite** is essential!

TAKE 1 CIABATTA LOAF AND POP IT IN A HOT OVEN FOR 5 MINUTES. SLICE IT IN HALF LENGTHWAYS. SPREAD THE BASE WITH **MARMITE** THEN ADD SOME CRUNCHY LETTUCE LEAVES, SOME SLICED TOMATOES, SOME THINLY SLICED FETA CHEESE AND SOME CHOPPED-UP PITTED OLIVES. DRIZZLE WITH A LITTLE OLIVE OIL, PUT THE LID BACK ON AND CUT ACROSS INTO 4 PORTIONS. HEY PRESTO: INSTANT CIABATTA SANDWICH!

Nineteen

ROASTIES

★

The best part of roast dinner just got better.

Roast potatoes are one of those vegetables that are just crying out for **Marmite**. Once you've cooked your roasties with it you will never look back.

ALLOW 2 MEDIUM POTATOES PER PERSON. PEEL AND CUT EACH POTATO INTO 4 AND BOIL IN SALTED WATER UNTIL THE EDGES BEGIN TO SOFTEN. DRAIN IN A COLANDER. PREHEAT THE OVEN TO 200C/GAS 6. MELT 40G OF BUTTER AND 3 TABLESPOONS OF VEGETABLE OIL IN A ROASTING TIN OVER A HOB AND STIR IN 1 TABLESPOON OF **MARMITE**. WHEN SIZZLING, ADD 1 MEDIUM ONION (SLICED), 1 DICED CLOVE OF GARLIC, A FEW SPRIGS OF ROSEMARY AND THEN TIP IN THE POTATOES. TURN IT ALL OVER IN THE BUTTERY MIXTURE AND ROAST IN THE OVEN FOR 1 HOUR. PERFECTION.

Twenty

CANAPÉS

★

Party on.

Here is an easy way to make instant vehicles for munchies if friends turn up unannounced.

TAKE A STALE BAGUETTE AND SLICE INTO ROUNDS ABOUT 1CM THICK, OR USE A STALE LOAF, SLICE, TAKE OFF THE CRUSTS AND CUT INTO SQUARES. WARM A LITTLE OLIVE OIL IN A SAUCEPAN AND STIR IN A TEASPOON OF **MARMITE**. BRUSH BOTH SIDES OF THE BREAD WITH THE OIL AND POP INTO THE OVEN AT 200C/GAS 6 FOR 5 MINUTES UNTIL GOLDEN. TOP WITH WHATEVER YOU FANCY – EGG MAYONNAISE, OR CREAM CHEESE AND CHIVES, OR HUMMUS OR WHATEVER ELSE YOU HAVE TO HAND.

Twenty-one

PÂTÉ

★

The incredible spreadable.

This is a quick, easy and very tasty pâté.
It takes an hour to set and minutes to devour
with warm crusty bread.

IN A BOWL, BEAT TOGETHER 200G OF CREAM CHEESE WITH 1 TEASPOON OF **MARMITE**. ADD IN 2 SPRING ONIONS AND 2 STICKS OF CELERY (BOTH VERY FINELY CHOPPED), THEN 100G OF GRATED CHEDDAR, A PINCH OF CAYENNE PEPPER, 100G OF CHOPPED CASHEW NUTS AND A TABLESPOON OF CHOPPED FRESH PARSLEY. MIX ALL THE INGREDIENTS TOGETHER WELL AND THEN TASTE AND SEASON WITH SALT AND GROUND BLACK PEPPER AS DESIRED. WARM SOME CRUSTY BREAD IN THE OVEN AND THEN TEAR AND DIP IT INTO YOUR SUMPTUOUS NUTTY PÂTÉ.

Twenty-two

BEANS

★

Take it slooooooooooow.

This is sort of the way the Greeks cook their green beans – long, slow and full of flavour. Not for the *al dente* lovers amongst you!

TO FEED 4 PEOPLE AS A SIDE DISH, TOP AND TAIL 500G OF FINE GREEN BEANS AND ADD TO A PAN OF BOILING WATER. COOK FOR 8 MINUTES AND DRAIN, KEEPING JUST A LITTLE WATER IN THE PAN. ADD TO THIS 2 TEASPOONS OF **MARMITE** AND THEN RETURN THE BEANS TO THE PAN. TIP IN A 400G TIN OF CHOPPED TOMATOES, SEASON WITH A TEASPOON OF DRIED HERBS AND SOME BLACK PEPPER AND COOK OVER A LOW HEAT FOR 30 MINUTES, MOVING THE BEANS GENTLY FROM TIME TO TIME AND THEN THEY ARE READY TO ENJOY.

Twenty-three

ONIONS

★

You'll be crying tears of joy.

This is a great fun way to cook onions and is so simple. The end result is great with sausages, chicken drumsticks – in fact anything you like.

FOR EACH PERSON, SLICE THE TOP OFF A MEDIUM-SIZED ONION AND A SLITHER OFF THE BASE SO IT WILL SIT ON A LINED BAKING TRAY AND HOLD TOGETHER. PEEL THE ONION AND THEN CUT THREE-QUARTERS OF THE WAY DOWN FROM THE TOP WITHOUT CUTTING THROUGH THE BASE. REPEAT THIS THREE MORE TIMES SO THAT YOU HAVE WHAT LOOKS LIKE A CLOSED FLOWER. EASE THE ONION APART ENOUGH TO DROP OR SQUEEZE A TEASPOON OF **MARMITE** INTO THE CENTRE. SEASON WITH BROWN SUGAR AND BLACK PEPPER. BAKE IN THE OVEN AT 180C/GAS 4 FOR 45 MINUTES OR UNTIL THE ONION FLOWER IS SOFT BUT CRISPY ON THE EDGE OF THE 'PETALS'.

Twenty-four

VINAIGRETTE

★

A drizzle of delight.

Making your own vinaigrette is so simple –
all you need is a whizzy machine and you'll
never suffer a bland salad again.

FOR A FAMILY SALAD, MEASURE INTO
A JUG 5 DESSERTSPOONS OF MALT
VINEGAR, 9 DESSERTSPOONS OF OLIVE
OIL, 1 HEAPED TEASPOON OF FRENCH
MUSTARD, 1 TEASPOON OF **MARMITE**
AND 1 TEASPOON OF RUNNY HONEY.
ADD A GOOD GRIND OF BLACK PEPPER
AND BLITZ – IT'S AS EASY AS THAT TO
MAKE BRILLIANT DRESSING FOR
YOUR SALAD.

Twenty-five

❧ POPCORN ❧

★

Lights. Camera. Marmite. Action!

Popcorn is such fun to make and all the family can get involved. If you like buttery **Marmite** toast then you'll love this.

AS A SNACK FOR FOUR, USE 60G OF POPPING CORN, 2 TABLESPOONS OF SUNFLOWER OIL, 30G OF BUTTER AND 1 TEASPOON OF **MARMITE**. LINE A BAKING TRAY WITH GREASEPROOF PAPER AND HEAT THE OVEN TO 160C/GAS 3. USING A HEAVY-BASED PAN, HEAT THE OIL AND WHEN HOT ADD THE CORN. COVER AND WAIT FOR THE POPPING, SHAKING THE PAN OCCASIONALLY. WHEN THE POPS ARE FAIRLY CONSTANT, TIP THEM INTO A BOWL. WARM THE BUTTER AND STIR IN THE MARMITE, THEN POUR IT ALL OVER THE POPCORN AND STIR UNTIL COATED. TIP ONTO THE BAKING TRAY AND POP IN THE OVEN FOR 5 MINUTES TO CRISP IT UP.

Twenty-six

PITTA

★

Pity the fool who doesn't love this sandwhich.

Pitta breads are perfectly formed pockets just waiting to be filled. Simply slice a sliver off along the long edge and pop it cut side down into a toaster for 30 seconds to warm it and open up the pocket.

FOR 2 PEOPLE, ROUGHLY CHOP 2 LARGE RIPE TOMATOES, A CHUNK OF CUCUMBER, HALF A SWEET RED PEPPER, HALF A SMALL RED ONION AND PUT INTO A BOWL. ADD SOME CHOPPED PARSLEY, CHOPPED CORIANDER, BLACK PEPPER, A DASH OF TABASCO AND SOME LIME JUICE. STIR THE WHOLE LOT TOGETHER. SPREAD THE INSIDE OF 2 WARMED PITTA BREADS WITH **MARMITE** AND THEN PILE IN THE SALSA – IT'S A WHOLE NEW TAKE ON A SALAD SANDWICH.

Twenty-seven
PANCAKES

★

Flippin' marvellous.

Try something completely different: these American-style pancakes served in a stack. Add bacon, banana and maple syrup for a real Stateside treat.

SIFT 250G OF SELF-RAISING FLOUR WITH HALF A TEASPOON OF BAKING POWDER INTO A BOWL. ADD 25G OF CASTER SUGAR, 2 EGGS AND WHISK WITH 275ML OF MILK. ADD 1 TEASPOON OF **MARMITE** MELTED IN 50G OF BUTTER AND WHISK AGAIN TO A THICK CREAMY MIXTURE. HEAT A HEAVY-BASED FRYING PAN WITH A LITTLE OIL AND DOLLOP A COUPLE OF TABLESPOONS OF BATTER INTO THE PAN FORMING A ROUND OF ABOUT 10CM. WHEN BUBBLES APPEAR, FLIP OVER AND COOK FOR A COUPLE MORE MINUTES UNTIL BOTH SIDES ARE FIRM AND JUST GOLDEN. CARRY ON UNTIL ALL THE MIXTURE IS USED AND SERVE IN WARM STACKS.

Twenty-eight

BURGERS

★

You'll have no beef with this recipe.

This is one to get the kids involved with because it gets messy. Making your own burgers is very satisfying and at least you know what's in them.

INTO A LARGE BOWL, PUT THE FOLLOWING: 500G OF LEAN MINCED BEEF, 1 MEDIUM ONION (GRATED), 1 EGG, 1 TEASPOON OF TOMATO KETCHUP, 1 TEASPOON OF DIJON MUSTARD, 1 TEASPOON OF **MARMITE**, HALF A TEASPOON OF MIXED HERBS AND BLACK PEPPER. NOW, GET YOUR HANDS IN AND SQUIDGE THE MIXTURE TO MIX IT ALL TOGETHER. SPRINKLE OVER A TABLESPOON OF FLOUR, MIX AND THEN FORM INTO 4–6 BURGERS. CHILL IN THE FRIDGE FOR 2 HOURS TO SET. COOK THE BURGERS TO YOUR TASTE OR FREEZE FOR AN INSTANT SUPPER ANOTHER DAY.

Twenty-nine

FRENCH
TOAST

★

C'est magnifique!

As most French people don't like **Marmite**,
perhaps we should call this very English eggy bread.
Any which way: *c'est délicieusement bon.*

FOR 2 PEOPLE, TAKE 2 THICK SLICES OF
GOOD RUSTIC BREAD AND SPREAD BOTH
SLICES ON BOTH SIDES WITH A THIN
SPREAD OF **MARMITE**. WHISK 2 EGGS
IN A SHALLOW DISH. MELT A KNOB
OF BUTTER AND A LITTLE OIL IN A
FRYING PAN UNTIL JUST SIZZLING.
DIP THE BREAD IN THE EGG AND FRY
UNTIL GOLDEN ON BOTH SIDES.
GREAT ON ITS OWN OR WITH YOUR
FAVOURITE BREAKFAST ACCOMPANIMENTS.

Thrity

RAREBIT

★

Cheese-tastic.

Cheese on toast is a highly underrated snack. Add some **Marmite** and an egg and you have an instant meal for very little time or money.

FOR EACH PERSON, TOAST A SLICE OF BREAD. THEN SPREAD WITH BUTTER AND **MARMITE** AND TOP WITH A HANDFUL OF GRATED CHEDDAR. SPRINKLE WITH A DASH OF WORCESTERSHIRE SAUCE AND POP UNDER THE GRILL. POACH AN EGG FOR EACH PERSON AND LAY IT ON THE MELTED CHEESY TOAST – SIMPLE.

Thirty-one

PASTA

★

Well and truly puts the 'Oooh' into umami.

An intensely flavoursome sauce that transforms a simple spaghetti dish. Be sure to use unsalted butter and do not salt the pasta water.

FEED 4 HUNGRY MOUTHS BY COOKING 350G OF DRIED SPAGHETTI ACCORDING TO PACK INSTRUCTIONS. MEANWHILE, MELT 50G OF UNSALTED BUTTER IN A SEPARATE SAUCEPAN AND STIR IN A TEASPOON OF **MARMITE**. MIX WELL UNTIL DISSOLVED. WHEN THE PASTA IS COOKED, DRAIN, RESERVING A LADLEFUL OF WATER TO STIR INTO THE MARMITE BUTTER MIX. POUR THE MIXTURE OVER THE SPAGHETTI, ADD A HEARTY HELPING OF GRATED PARMESAN AND EAT IMMEDIATELY.

Thirty-two

TOFU

★

Tofu or not tofu? That is the question.

Tofu is not big on flavour on its own so a curry is a great way to pep it up. This will satisfy 4 hungry people.

HEAT 2 TABLESPOONS OF VEGETABLE OIL IN A HEAVY-BASED SAUCEPAN AND STIR IN 2 TABLESPOONS OF CURRY PASTE AND 1 TEASPOON OF **MARMITE**. DICE 1 LARGE ONION. FINELY CHOP 2 CLOVES OF GARLIC AND PEEL AND CUBE 1 LARGE SWEET POTATO AND ADD TO THE PAN. KEEP EVERYTHING MOVING IN THE PAN AND WHEN GOLDEN ADD A 400G TIN OF CHOPPED TOMATOES. WHEN THE SWEET POTATOES ARE HALFWAY COOKED ADD IN THE TOFU (WHICH YOU'LL NEED TO HAVE RINSED, DRAINED AND CUBED). COOK GENTLY, ADDING A LITTLE WATER IF TOO DRY, FOR 20 MINUTES OR UNTIL THE POTATO IS TENDER. SEASON AND SERVE WITH RICE AND CHOPPED FRESH CORIANDER.

Thirty-three
{ SOUP }
★

Ladlefuls of Marmitey goodness.

French onion soup is traditionally made with beef stock but thanks to our mate **Marmite**, you can create a delicious vegetarian alternative.

HEAT 2 TABLESPOONS OF OLIVE OIL WITH 50G OF BUTTER IN A HEAVY-BASED PAN UNTIL VERY HOT. ADD 750G OF SLICED ONIONS, A FINELY DICED CLOVE OF GARLIC AND A TEASPOON OF BROWN SUGAR AND COOK UNTIL DARK GOLDEN. TURN DOWN THE HEAT TO VERY LOW AND LEAVE COOKING FOR 30 MINUTES. NEXT, ADD 1.5 LITRES OF WATER, 250ML OF WHITE WINE AND A TABLESPOON OF **MARMITE**. SCRAPE ALL THE DARK GOODIES FROM THE BASE OF THE PAN, SEASON AS REQUIRED AND LEAVE TO COOK GENTLY FOR 1 HOUR. SERVE WITH FLOATING CROUTONS OOZING WITH MELTED CHEESE.

Thirty-four

MUSHROOMS

★

A salad truly worth foraging for.

You can use any sort of mushrooms for this scrummy salad. Field mushrooms are great, chestnut mushrooms are better and mixed wild mushrooms are divine.

AS A SIDE DISH FOR 4, SLICE 250G OF MUSHROOMS INTO A BOWL AND ADD 2 CRUSHED CLOVES OF GARLIC, 2 HEAPED TABLESPOONS OF CHOPPED FRESH PARSLEY AND SEVERAL GOOD GRINDS OF BLACK PEPPER. WHISK 200ML OF EXTRA-VIRGIN OLIVE WITH 1 TEASPOON OF **MARMITE** AND 2 TEASPOONS OF WHITE WINE VINEGAR. POUR THIS OVER THE MUSHROOMS AND TURN THEM ALL GENTLY TO COAT. COVER AND CHILL FOR 2 HOURS, TURNING OCCASIONALLY. BRING BACK TO ROOM TEMPERATURE AND SERVE.

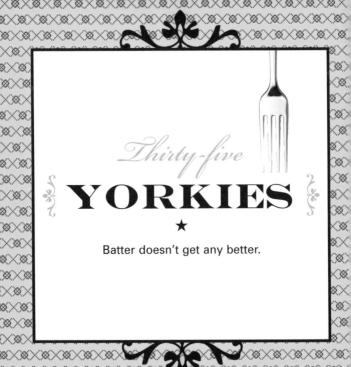

Thirty-five

YORKIES

★

Batter doesn't get any better.

Making you own Yorkshire puddings is so easy. Make a batch or two for the freezer too by following this recipe. The **Marmite** makes them extra-crispy.

PREHEAT YOUR OVEN TO 220C/GAS 7 AND SLIDE IN A 12-HOLE YORKSHIRE TIN WITH A LITTLE OIL INSIDE EACH WELL. LEAVE FOR AT LEAST FIVE MINUTES TO ALLOW THE TIN TO GET REALLY HOT. SIFT 175G OF PLAIN FLOUR INTO A BOWL, CRACK IN 5 EGGS AND GRADUALLY WHISK IN 150ML EACH OF MILK AND SPARKLING WATER FOLLOWED BY A TEASPOON OF **MARMITE**. CAREFULLY REMOVE THE YORKIE TIN AND POUR THE MIXTURE VERY QUICKLY INTO THE WELLS AND THEN IMMEDIATELY RETURN TO THE OVEN. ROAST FOR 20 MINUTES UNTIL GOLDEN AND CRISPY ROUND THE TOPS. (MAKES 36 YORKIES)

Thirty-six

CROUTONS

★

Give salads and soups some crunch.

Croutons are one of the best ways to finish a salad. By adding **Marmite** you will have a really savoury flavour too.

SLICE SOME STALE BREAD AND CUT INTO 2CM CUBES. COAT THE BASE OF A ROASTING TIN WITH OLIVE OIL AND HEAT IN THE OVEN AT 180C/GAS 4 FOR 5 MINUTES. BRING OUT THE TIN AND STIR IN A TEASPOON OF **MARMITE**. TOSS IN A GOOD HANDFUL OF BREAD CUBES AND TURN IN THE OIL. RETURN THE TIN TO THE OVEN AND COOK FOR 10 MINUTES UNTIL GOLDEN AND CRUNCHY. DRAIN ON KITCHEN PAPER AND SCATTER OVER YOUR SALAD.

Thirty-seven

BANG BANG

★

Bang by name. Bang on those tastebuds.

The 'bang bang' comes from the chilli sauce and makes this a fun meal for using up leftover chicken or turkey. This sauce will be enough for 4-6 portions.

IN A BOWL, MIX TOGETHER THE FOLLOWING: 2 TEASPOONS OF SUNFLOWER OIL, 3 TABLESPOONS OF PEANUT BUTTER, 2 TABLESPOONS OF CHILLI SAUCE, 2 TEASPOONS OF **MARMITE**, 1 TABLESPOON OF CASTER SUGAR, 1 TABLESPOON OF WHITE WINE VINEGAR AND 3 TABLESPOONS OF WATER. JOB DONE, NOW FOR THE 'WOW' FACTOR. ON A BIG PLATTER, ARRANGE SHREDDED CRUNCHY LETTUCE, SLICED CUCUMBER AND ROUGHLY CHOPPED MINT AND CORIANDER. MIX THE COLD SHREDDED MEAT WITH THE SAUCE AND TIP INTO THE CENTRE OF THE PLATTER, SAVING A LITTLE SAUCE TO DRIZZLE OVER THE SALAD.

Thirty-eight

SALSA

★

Get ready to rumba!

This is salsa with a difference. It's fresh herbs from the garden and goes wonderfully with fish.

ROUGHLY CHOP 15G EACH OF TARRAGON LEAVES, MINT LEAVES AND DILL FRONDS AND PUT THEM IN A BOWL. ADD A 10CM CHUNK OF FINELY DICED CUCUMBER AND 2 TEASPOONS OF FINELY CHOPPED GHERKIN. MIX BY GENTLY TURNING THE INGREDIENTS OVER IN THE BOWL. WHISK A TEASPOON OF **MARMITE** WITH 3 TABLESPOONS OF EXTRA-VIRGIN OLIVE OIL, THEN ADD THE JUICE OF HALF A LEMON. MIX TOGETHER AND FINALLY POUR OVER THE SALSA.

Thirty-nine

BAGELS

★

Runs rings round other brunches.

This is a monster bagel, which should satisfy a healthy appetite for brunch or lunch. Bagels deserve a classy filling and **Marmite** fits the bill.

SPLIT AND TOAST YOUR BAGEL AND SPREAD EACH HALF WITH A LITTLE BUTTER. SPREAD THE BASE WITH CREAM CHEESE, THEN **MARMITE** AND ARRANGE LAYERS OF PASTRAMI, SLICED RED ONION, TOMATO, AVOCADO AND CUCUMBER ON TOP OF THAT. SQUEEZE A LITTLE LEMON JUICE OVER AND REPLACE THE LID. THEN TUCK IN TO YOUR MONSTER BAGEL!

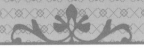

Forty

CRISPS

★

Snack to your heart's content.

Making your own crisps is great fun – but making your own **Marmite** crisps is magic.

HEAT A DEEP-FAT FRYER TO 190C. IN A SHALLOW DISH, MIX TOGETHER 1 TABLESPOON OF VEGETABLE OIL AND 1 TABLESPOON OF **MARMITE** UNTIL YOU HAVE A PASTE. TO MAKE ENOUGH TO SHARE, PEEL 1 LARGE POTATO AND THEN USE A POTATO PEELER TO PEEL OFF THIN ROUNDS TO MAKE THE CRISPS. RINSE AND PAT DRY TO REMOVE THE STARCH. PUT THE POTATO SLICES IN THE PASTE AND GET MESSY BY RUBBING THE GOO INTO THE POTATO SHAVINGS. FINALLY, DEEP-FRY FOR 3–4 MINUTES UNTIL DARK GOLDEN. DRAIN ON KITCHEN PAPER AND THEY WILL CRISP UP AS THEY COOL.

Picture credits

Paul Hartley

Paul Hartley is the bestselling author of
The Marmite Cookbook, *The Marmite World
Cookbook* and *The Little Book of Marmite Tips*
(all Absolute Press). He is a truly dedicated
(and unapologetic!) evangelist for the culinary
wonders of Marmite and his innovative powers with
this iconic storecupboard spread know no bounds.